I Am a Gymn

For my daughter Adriana,
You are so beautiful and talented.
I love you, Mom

Written and photographed by
Anjeanetta Prater Matthews

I like being a gymnast.

I go to the gym every day.

I do my exercises.

4

I walk on the balance beam.

I hang on the bars.

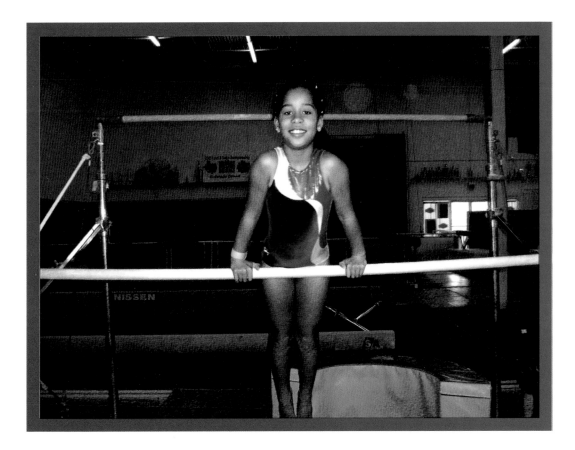

I jump on the trampoline.

10

I do flips.

I'm so tired and thirsty!

I'm going to drink

some water and then

I will go home.

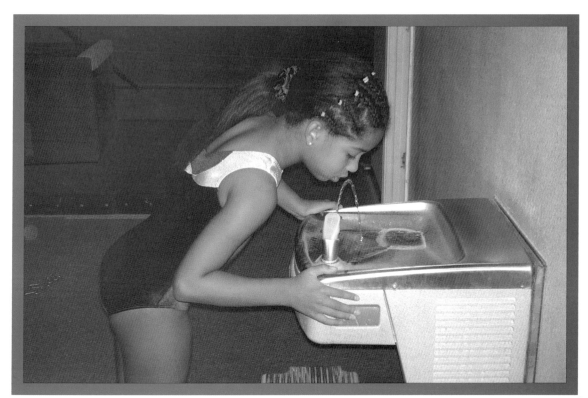